St. Seraphim's Beatitudes

Blessings for Our Path to Heaven
Based on the Life of the Wonderworker of Sarov

Illustrations by Paul Drozdowski
Text by Priest Daniel Marshall

St. Innocent Press
MIDDLEBURY, INDIANA

This book is published in memory of
the servant of God Michael Grigorieff (†2003),
an artist who loved children.

May his memory be eternal!

St. Seraphim's Beatitudes
Blessings for Our Path to Heaven
Based on the Life of the Wonderworker of Sarov

Published by St. Innocent Press
Post Office Box 1468, Middlebury, Indiana 46540
www.stinnocentpress.com

Printed in the United States of America

ISBN-13: 978-0-9786543-0-6

Publisher's Cataloging-in-Publication data

Marshall, Daniel William.
St. Seraphim's Beatitudes : blessings on our path to Heaven based on the life of the wonderworker of Sarov / Priest Daniel Marshall ; illustrated by Paul Drozdowski.
p. cm.
ISBN 978-0-9786543-0-6
Summary: This life of Venerable Seraphim of Sarov (1759–1833), a Russian Orthodox saint, illustrates Christian virtues through watercolors and short phrases based on Christ's Beatitudes.

1. Serafim, Sarovskii, Saint, 1759-1833. 2. Beatitudes. 3. Orthodox Eastern Church--Biography.
4. Spirituality--Orthodox Eastern Church. 5. Christian biography. 6. Christian saints--Russia--Biography. 7. Devotional literature. I. Drozdowski, Paul. II. Title.

BX597.S37 . M37 2008
248.4819319--dc22   2007906962

BLESSED ARE YOU WHEN YOU RECEIVE THE HOLY SPIRIT.

GREAT IS GOD'S LOVE FOR MANKIND. He wants all people to live in peace with Him forever in heaven and to enjoy His blessings in this life. This is why God the Father sent His Son, Jesus Christ, to save us and to teach us how to live. This is why He sends the Holy Spirit to give us life and to bless us.

The greatest members of Christ's Holy Orthodox Church are His saints. The lives of these saints, such as Venerable Seraphim of Sarov, show us how to live by God's law so that we can obtain His blessings.

St. Seraphim was born in 1759 in the town of Kursk, Russia. As an infant he was named Prokhor, though he is best known as Seraphim, the name given to him years later when he became a monk. Like every Orthodox Christian he received the gift of the Holy Spirit when he was Baptized and anointed with Holy Chrism. He struggled to love God and his neighbor throughout his life so that he would acquire more of this grace of the Holy Spirit.

3

BLESSED ARE YOU WHEN YOU TRUST IN THE LORD.

PROKHOR BECAME VERY SICK when he was ten years old. He and his mother both prayed to God for help. Then the Mother of God appeared to Prokhor in a vision and promised to heal him. In his town there was a miracle-working icon of the Mother of God known as the Kursk-Root Icon. During a festal procession, this holy icon passed by Prokhor's home. His mother carried him to venerate the icon. In answer to their prayers, the Mother of God fulfilled her promise and cured Prokhor.

Prokhor's love for the Lord and His Most-Pure Mother grew daily. Most of all, he enjoyed reading Holy Scripture and the lives of saints. When he was a young man, he decided to give his whole life to serving Our Savior Jesus Christ. Placing his full trust in the Lord, Prokhor received his mother's blessing to join a monastery.

BLESSED ARE YOU WHEN YOU ARE OBEDIENT.

P ROKHOR ENTERED SAROV MONASTERY when he was nineteen years old. Wise, experienced monks taught him how to bake church bread, to work as a carpenter, and to sing in church. Most importantly, they taught him to pray.

He did what his spiritual father told him, just as a child obeys his father and mother. St. Seraphim said, "There is nothing greater than obedience."

When he was twenty-seven years old, he chose to live the rest of his life in Sarov Monastery. He became a monk and was given a new name: Seraphim. This is the same name given to the angels who serve at the Lord's throne.

ЦРЬ СЛВЬ

ІС ХС

НІ КА

К Т

ГА ГГ

МЛРБ

7

BLESSED ARE YOU WHEN YOU LOVE THE CHURCH.

S<small>T. S</small>ERAPHIM LOVED NOTHING MORE THAN TO BE IN CHURCH. After he was ordained a deacon, it gave him great joy to serve close to the holy altar table. "The Lord Himself is present here," said St. Seraphim. "All the Cherubim and Seraphim, and all the heavenly Powers surround Him, trembling." St. Seraphim knew this to be true because once during the Divine Liturgy he saw a vision of the Lord Jesus Christ Himself entering the holy altar surrounded by a host of angels.

BLESSED ARE YOU WHEN YOU TAKE UP YOUR CROSS.

Our Savior Jesus Christ told his disciples: *Whosoever will come after Me, let him deny himself, and take up his cross and follow Me.* By His precious Cross, the Lord defeated the Devil and his demons. St. Seraphim took up his cross by leaving his family, friends, and his home to follow Christ as a monk in Sarov Monastery.

Just as Christ often prayed in solitude, St. Seraphim moved to a small hut in the woods near the monastery so he could devote himself wholly to prayer. He prayed that God's grace would help him overcome the evil forces which try to separate man from God. For a thousand days and nights he prayed while kneeling on a rock.

Blessed are you when you suffer for the Lord.

Three men once demanded money of St. Seraphim. He told them that he had none. The men did not believe him and in anger beat him until he was almost dead. All they found in his cell were a few potatoes and a sack with stones on which he slept. St. Seraphim managed eventually to drag himself to the monastery for help.

While doctors examined him, the Mother of God appeared to him along with the Apostle Peter and St. John the Evangelist. St. Seraphim heard her ask why the doctors were troubling themselves. Then she pointed at St. Seraphim and told St. John, "He is one of ours." After the vision, St. Seraphim was filled with great joy. He began to feel better.

Healed by the Mother of God, St. Seraphim regained his strength and returned to live in the woods. He insisted that the men not be punished. Later, they begged him for forgiveness. In the end, poor health forced St. Seraphim to return to Sarov Monastery. He had lived alone in the woods for fifteen years.

BLESSED ARE YOU WHEN YOU LOVE YOUR NEIGHBOR.

St. Seraphim accepted no visitors for the first five years after he resumed living in Sarov Monastery. He only left his cell for church. Then the Mother of God told him to end his seclusion. She reminded him of Jesus Christ's words: *Neither do men light a candle, and put it under a bushel, but on a candlestick. Let your light so shine before men, that they may see your good works, and glorify your Father, which is in heaven.* After many years of spiritual struggle, St. Seraphim was full of the light of the Holy Spirit. He began to accept visitors, providing comfort and instruction to all.

Michael Manturov was one such visitor. His legs were so diseased that he could barely walk. Finding no cure from doctors, this young man asked St. Seraphim to help. "My joy!" he replied. "Believe that the Lord will heal you, and I, wretched Seraphim, will pray." He prayed before his icon of the Mother of God and then anointed Manturov with oil from the lamp which burned in front of it. "With the grace given to me by the Lord," said St. Seraphim, "you are the first person I heal."

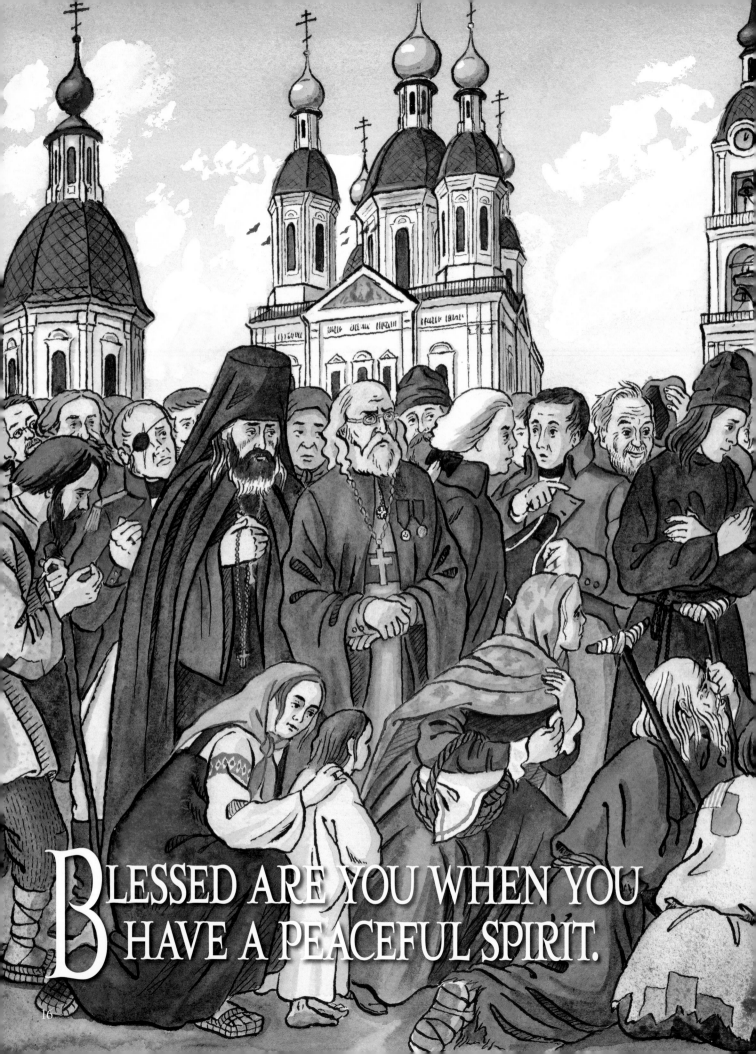

BLESSED ARE YOU WHEN YOU HAVE A PEACEFUL SPIRIT.

News of Manturov's healing spread throughout Russia. Pilgrims flocked to St. Seraphim for prayers and advice. "I implore you to acquire a peaceful spirit," he said, "and then thousands of souls around you will be saved."

BLESSED ARE YOU WHEN YOU PRAY FOR OTHERS.

HOLY SCRIPTURE TEACHES US TO PRAY without ceasing. When we ask that God be merciful to our family, friends, and acquaintances, we are fulfilling Christ's command to love our neighbors as we love ourselves. "Every good work, done for Christ's sake, gives us the gifts of the Holy Spirit," taught St. Seraphim. "But prayer produces the Holy Spirit most of all, and it is the easiest for everyone to practice."

It makes no difference if we are healthy or sick, rich or poor, happy or sad, we are always able to pray. He advised everyone to pray, fast, and follow God's law of love for the sake of acquiring the Holy Spirit. St. Seraphim prayed every day for the thousands of pilgrims who visited him and for those who sent him letters asking for prayers. His prayers drew him closer to God. He was even seen to rise off the ground while praying.

BLESSED ARE YOU
WHEN YOU
BELIEVE IN
HEAVEN.

G OD CREATED MAN TO LIVE WITH HIM for eternity. We Christians struggle to live a God-pleasing life on earth so that we might live with God forever in heaven. "If only you knew," St. Seraphim once told another monk, "what joy, what sweetness awaits the righteous in heaven."

True peace and love abound in heaven, as it once did in the Garden of Eden. Adam and Eve lived in harmony with all the animals while they were there. They were friends with lions, wolves, and bears. The righteous often enjoy a taste of heavenly blessedness while still on earth. So much of the grace of the Holy Spirit had been given to St. Seraphim that all the animals were friendly to him, as they had once been to Adam and Eve in the Garden of Eden. He even fed bread from his hand to bears and other wild animals.

BLESSED ARE YOU WHEN YOU TURN TO THE MOTHER OF GOD.

St. Seraphim loved the Mother of God greatly. He often prayed before his favorite icon of the Theotokos, the Icon of Tender Mercy. Whenever he turned in prayer to our Lord's Most-Holy Mother, she would help him. She often appeared to him in visions.

She instructed him how to guide the nuns of Diveyevo Convent, a community near Sarov for which St. Seraphim was responsible. The Mother of God claimed Diveyevo as her own special territory. She told him to build a windmill for grinding grain at the convent and to surround part of the convent with an earthen embankment. Once, he saw a vision in which the Mother of God touched her staff to the ground, causing a miracle-working spring to flow forth.

S**T. S**ERAPHIM **STRUGGLED** to do the work of the Lord always. As their spiritual father, he guided the nuns in Diveyevo to salvation. He arranged to construct the wind-powered mill. He obeyed the instruction given to him by the Mother of God in a vision and told the nuns to build the embankment around the convent.

The nuns, busy with other jobs, did not begin work on the embankment. One night, a nun saw St. Seraphim digging by candlelight. She fell at his feet, asking forgiveness for not being obedient. When she looked up, he had disappeared, but his pickaxe was still there. Wondrously, St. Seraphim had been in his cell all night!

A strong wind once turned the mill's grindstones very quickly. The nun working in the mill could not pour enough grain between the stones to prevent them from becoming dangerously hot. In fear, she threw herself on them and called for St. Seraphim to help, though he was far away in his cell. St. Seraphim instantly appeared and stopped the grindstones. "My child, did you call out for me?" asked St. Seraphim. "I am always with those who call on me for help."

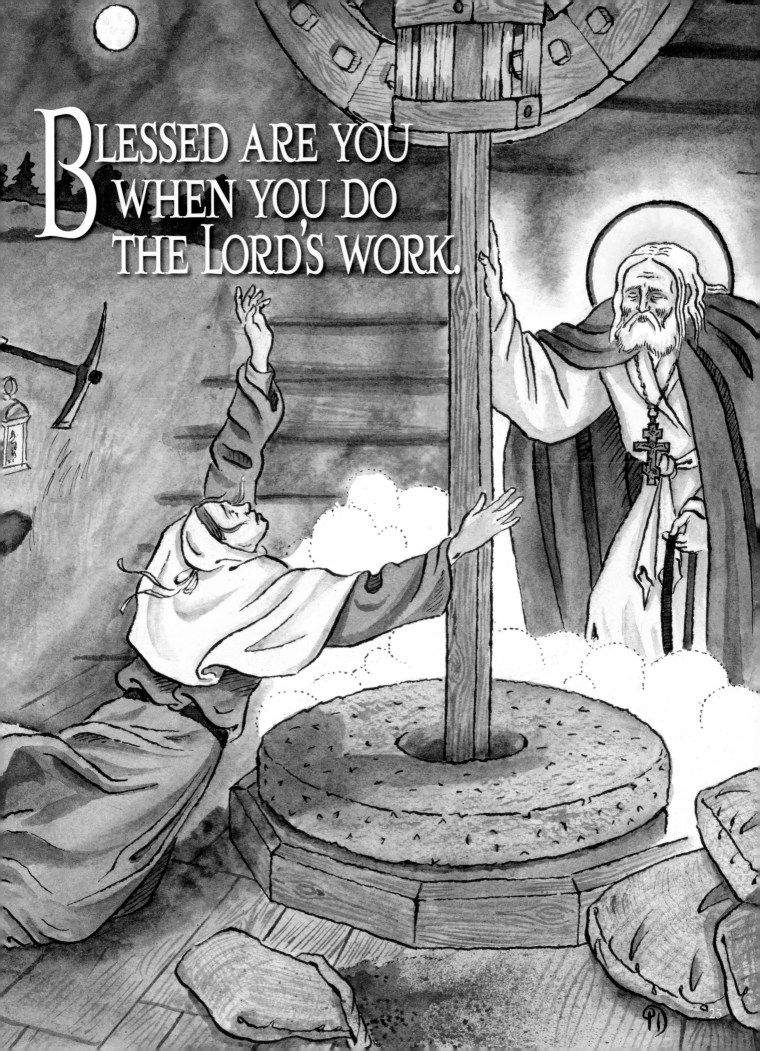

BLESSED ARE YOU
WHEN YOU DO
THE LORD'S WORK.

BLESSED ARE YOU WHEN YOU HAVE STRONG FAITH.

B<small>Y</small> G<small>OD'S</small> <small>GRACE,</small> St. Seraphim helped those who approached him with faith in the Lord. Nikolai Motovilov was one such man. He had been so ill that for more than three years he had not been out of bed. One day five men carried him to St. Seraphim. "Do you believe," asked St. Seraphim, "that the Lord, just as He used to heal instantly and by His word alone, can today just as easily and instantly heal those asking for help by His word alone?"

"I truly believe all of this with my whole soul and heart," answered Motovilov.

"If you believe," said St. Seraphim, "then you are healed already!" By God's grace, Motovilov stood upright and walked on his own for the first time in years.

Blessed are you when you acquire the Holy Spirit.

MOTOVILOV ONCE DISCUSSED THE PURPOSE OF LIFE with St. Seraphim. "The true goal of our life as Christians is the acquisition of the Holy Spirit." St. Seraphim explained that fasting, prayer, attending church, and all other good works done for Jesus Christ's sake serve as the means to acquire more of the grace of the Holy Spirit.

The grace of the Holy Spirit is spiritual light which illumines us. To prove this, St. Seraphim prayed that God allow Motovilov to see with his physical eyes the spiritual light of the Holy Spirit. He saw an incredible light bursting forth from within St. Seraphim. St. Seraphim also saw this same light coming from Motovilov. Motovilov felt great warmth, abundant joy, and true peace within himself. Christ spoke of these gifts of the Holy Spirit when He said, *Behold the Kingdom of God is within you.*

BLESSED ARE
YOU WHEN
YOU ARE CALLED
TO THE LORD.

BY HIS RESURRECTION FROM THE DEAD, Christ restored to us all the chance for a life of eternal blessedness after our souls depart from our bodies at death. This great good news inspired St. Seraphim to welcome all his visitors with the Paschal greeting: "My joy! Christ is Risen!"

St. Seraphim had no fear of death. Christ's resurrection made him sure of eternal life. He said, "What joy, what delight overwhelms the soul of a righteous man, when, after its separation from the body, angels greet it and present it before the Face of God."

On the morning of January 2, 1833, a passing monk noticed smoke in St. Seraphim's cell. Entering, he found the body of the saint kneeling before his icon of the Mother of God of Tender Mercy. Angels had already taken his soul to God.

BLESSED ARE YOU WHEN YOU GLORIFY GOD'S SAINTS.

PRECIOUS IN THE SIGHT OF THE LORD IS THE DEATH OF HIS SAINTS, proclaims King David in his Psalter. These words could have been written about St. Seraphim. Tsar-Martyr Nicholas and thousands of the faithful shared these sentiments at St. Seraphim's glorification on July 19, 1903.

To this day, St. Seraphim looks down from heaven on our troubled world and answers the prayers of those who cry out to him. He promised this himself, saying, "All that troubles your soul, whatever has happened—tell me everything. I will hear you and all your grief will subside! Speak with me as you did when I was living. For you, I am alive and always will be!"

O Venerable Father Seraphim, pray to God for us!